# Look at That Building!
## A First Book of Structures

**Scot Ritchie**

Kids Can Press

Dedicated to my dad, Ross Ritchie,
one of Canada's great architects — S.R.

Kids Can Press gratefully acknowledges the financial support of the Government of Ontario, through the Ontario Media Development Corporation; the Ontario Arts Council; the Canada Council for the Arts; and the Government of Canada, through the CBF, for our publishing activity.

Published in Canada and the U.S. by Kids Can Press Ltd.
25 Dockside Drive, Toronto, ON  M5A 0B5

Kids Can Press is a Corus Entertainment Inc. company

www.kidscanpress.com

Edited by Samantha Swenson
Designed by Julia Naimska

Printed and bound in Malaysia in 5/2017 by Tien Wah Press (Pte.) Ltd.

CM 11  0 9 8 7 6 5 4

**Library and Archives Canada Cataloguing in Publication**

Ritchie, Scot
     Look at that building! : a first book of structures / Scot Ritchie.

Includes index.
ISBN 978-1-55453-696-2

1. Building — Juvenile literature.  I. Title.

TH149.R58 2011        j690        C2011-901076-3

# Contents

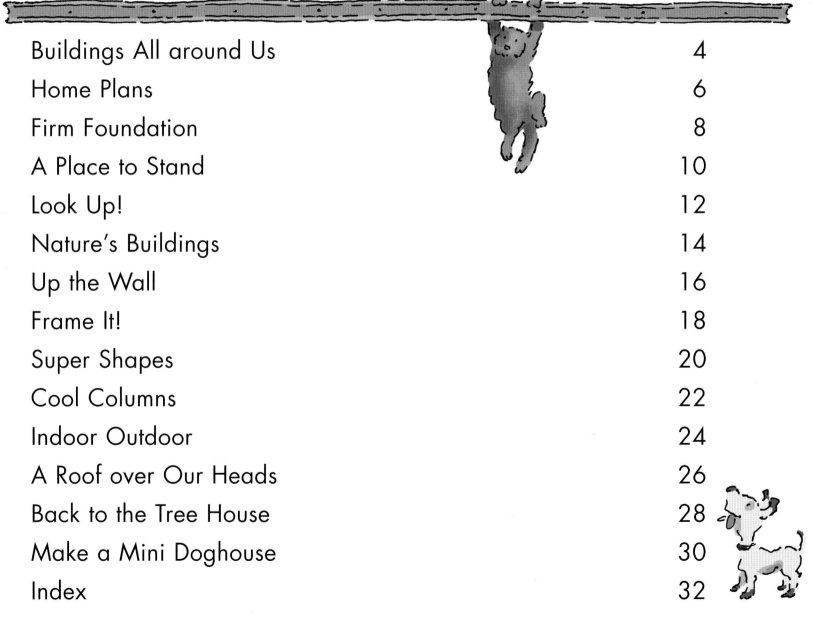

# Buildings All around Us

You've probably noticed that your house has floors, walls and windows. But did you know it might have a foundation, a frame and beams, too? Let's go for a walk with our five friends to find out about how buildings are put together.

Martin

Nick

Yulee

Max

Pedro

Sally

Ollie

**A building is a structure: something that is made of different parts. Buildings are all around us and have lots of different uses.**

# Home Plans

Sally's dad has built her a tree house. Her friends have come over to see it. What a great little building! Everybody is having fun except Max. He can't climb up to join them.

**People build everywhere: on the water, on top of cliffs, in trees and even underground!**

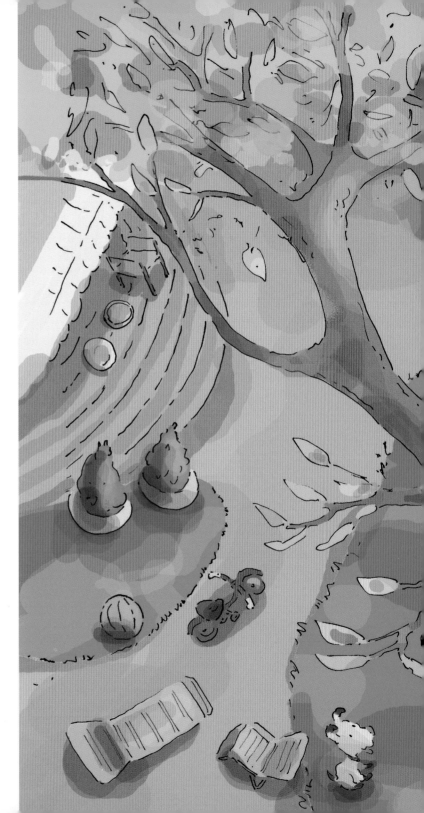

# Firm Foundation

Yulee thinks that such a deep hole must have taken a lot of digging. Martin is watching the construction workers pour concrete. This foundation is going to be very strong.

A foundation is the lowest part of a building. It keeps the rest of the building stable by anchoring it securely in the ground.

**The taller a building is, the deeper and larger its foundation has to be. Some skyscrapers' foundations go four floors underground!**

# A Place to Stand

Next stop: the library! Pedro is making sure the floor is solid enough to hold all these books.

A floor is the surface we stand on in a building. Floors are made of a very durable material so that they last a long time.

**Floors can be made from many different materials, including wood, stone, dirt and concrete.**

# Look Up!

As they leave the library, Nick notices the beams above his head. They are wide and very long. How many beams can you see?

A beam is usually a long, thick piece of wood, stone or metal. It is very rigid so that it can support floors, ceilings and other building parts. You can't always see the beams, but most structures have them.

**The first beams were probably made from tree trunks.**

# Nature's Buildings

Some animals build their own homes. Too bad Max can't build his own doghouse! Yulee decides they will just have to do a great job for him.

To make their nests, wasps chew tiny bits of wood into a pulp. Then they spit out the pulp and pat it into place with their feet. When it hardens, they have a waterproof home!

Most birds make nests, too. They use twigs, leaves and sometimes even spider webs. They weave the materials together to make a place to raise their young. What other animal homes can you see?

# Up the Wall

Yulee looks in a window at her school. She read at the library that walls do more than just hold up the blackboard.

Walls do many important things. They divide a building into rooms and keep the outside … outside. They also help keep the roof up.

**Ancient castle walls were made of stone. They could be 6 meters (20 feet) thick!**

# Frame It!

Pedro looks up at the skyscrapers. He can see right through one of them because it is just being built. Pedro is looking at the building's frame.

Frames can be made of wood, steel or concrete. A frame gives the structure shape and support. Other parts, like beams and walls, are built on top of the frame.

**A frame is sort of like our skeleton. Without it, there would be nothing holding us up from the inside!**

# Super Shapes

Sally has been to the city hall before. She remembers the dome. Look how big it is!

Three shapes are used in a lot of buildings because they are so strong.

An **arch** is a structure that is curved at the top. The arch shape helps spread weight around.

A **dome** is also curved at the top and helps spread the weight of a structure. It can cover a large space with few supports.

A **triangle** is the strongest shape. Lots of weight can be added to a triangle and it won't change its shape.

# Cool Columns

The columns of this bus shelter remind Yulee of trees. They remind Nick of the columns on his porch at home.

Columns are used to hold up parts of a structure, such as the roof. Because they support so much weight, they have to be made of sturdy materials.

**Columns are like beams, except one is vertical and the other horizontal. They both provide support.**

# Indoor Outdoor

Sally loves to look in through the big windowed door at the fire station. The door lets light in and lets fire trucks out — in a hurry!

Most buildings have doors and windows. Doors allow people (and pets) to come and go. Windows allow light (or sometimes a nice breeze) to come in.

**Not all doors and windows are in the wall. Sometimes they are in the roof or even in the floor!**

# A Roof over Our Heads

It's raining — time to find somewhere dry. Martin suggests they go back to the tree fort. Pedro is glad they will have a roof protecting them.

A roof is the top covering of a building. It shelters the building from the weather.

**Some roofs have grass growing on them. They are called green roofs because they help the environment.**

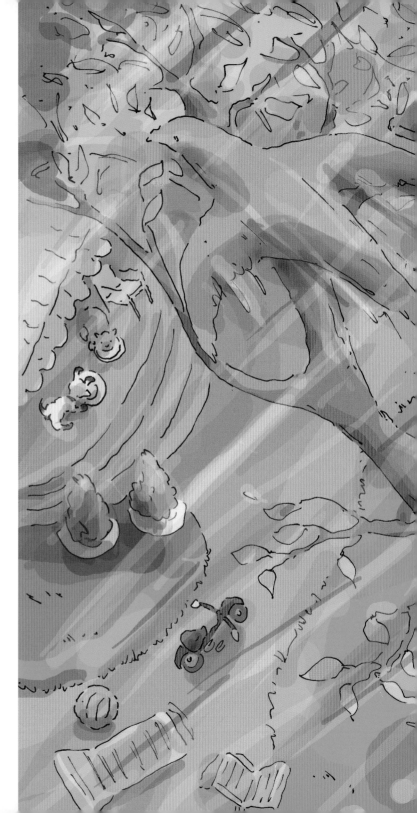

# Back to the Tree House

The gang is happy to be back at the cozy tree house. Max is still downstairs, keeping dry on the porch. Soon he will have a cozy house of his very own!

I can't wait to start building Max's doghouse.
I'm glad we found this book at the library. Now we know where to start.
Let's start with the foundation!

# Make a Mini Doghouse

Here's a plan for making a mini doghouse. You'll need: marshmallows, craft sticks, construction paper, scissors, glue and tape.

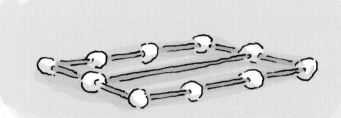

**Step 1:** Build a frame for the floor using marshmallows and wooden sticks.

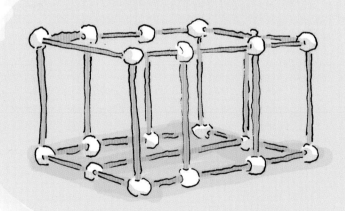

**Step 2:** Add the frame for the walls.

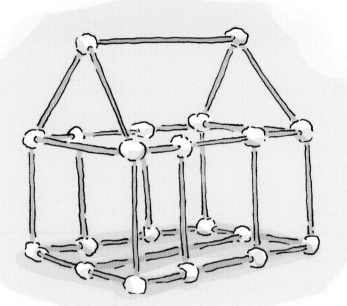

**Step 3:** Add a peak for the roof.

**Step 5:** Glue and tape the paper to the frame.

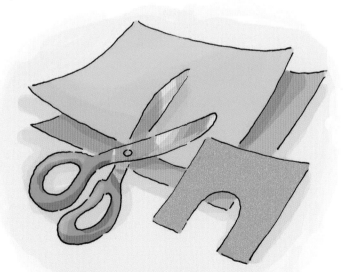

**Step 4:** Ask a parent to cut the paper to fit the roof and walls.

# Index